I0439817

United States Department of Agriculture
Forest Service

Pacific Southwest
Research Station

General Technical
Report
PSW-GTR-246

September 2013

Proceedings of the International Workshop on Monitoring Forest Degradation in Southeast Asia

November 13-14, 2012 – Bangkok, Thailand

Editors

Leif A. Mortenson is forest inventory specialist, US Department of Agriculture Forest Service, Pacific Northwest Research Station, 620 SW Main St. Suite 400, Portland, OR 97205 (email address: leifmortenson@fs.fed.us)

James J. Halperin is research forester, Center for International Forestry Research, Lusaka, Zambia (email: j halperin@cgiar.org)

Patricia N. Manley is conservation and biodiversity supervisory scientist, US Department of Agriculture Forest Service, Pacific Southwest Research Station, 2480 Carson Road, Placerville, CA 95667 (email: pmanley@fs fed.us)

Rick L. Turner is ecologist, US Department of Agriculture Forest Service, Tongass National Forest, 8510 Mendenhall Loop Road, Juneau, AK 99801 (email:rlturner@fs.fed.us)

Papers are provided by the authors in camera-ready form for printing. Authors are responsible for the content and accuracy. Opinions expressed may not necessarily reflect the position of the U.S. Department of Agriculture.

This GTR and all associated materials, including country level reports for Cambodia, Laos, and Vietnam, can be accessed at "http://www.leafasia.org/events/degradation-regional-workshop."

Cover photo: Houaphanh Province, Lao PDR by Leif Mortenson.

Proceedings of the International Workshop on Monitoring Forest Degradation in Southeast Asia

November 13-14, 2012 – Bangkok, Thailand

Leif A. Mortenson, James J. Halperin, Patricia N. Manley, and Rick L. Turner

Editors

U.S. Department of Agriculture, Forest Service
Pacific Southwest Research Station
Albany, CA
General Technical Report PSW-GTR-246
September 2013

Conference Sponsors

USDA Forest Service International Programs (USFS-IP)
USA International Development (USAID) – Asia
Lowering Emissions in Asia's Forests (LEAF)

We would like to acknowledge all of the preliminary work that went into crafting this workshop. There were numerous reviews of the agenda to ensure that the resulting workshop would truly meet the original goals for the Scope of Work. The workshop Steering Committee of David Ganz, Sandra Brown, and James Halperin is due special acknowledgement. Additionally, much effort was put into selecting and bringing together the appropriate experts from around the region and the world to present and participate in the workshop. The tireless coordination efforts of Ms. Elle Rattiya deserve a very large thank you. Thanks also go out to Peter Stephen, Jamie Halperin, Leif Mortenson, and Pat Manley for facilitating small group sessions, to Leif Mortenson and Nguyen Hanh Quyen for tirelessly taking notes during the entire workshop, and to all the participants for their active engagement that made this workshop a success. Our reviewers for this GTR, Thomas Brandeis, Beth Lebow and Gabriel Eickhoff contributed extremely valuable suggestions for improving the document

Abstract

Mortenson, Leif A.; Halperin, James J.; Manley, Patricia N.; Turner, Rich L. 2013
Proceedings of the international workshop on monitoring forest degradation in Southeast Asia. Gen. Tech. Rep. PSW-GTR-246. Albany, CA: U.S. Department of Agriculture, Forest Service, Pacific Southwest Research Station. 56 p.

The international workshop on monitoring forest degradation in Southeast Asia provided a forum for discussion of the technical, social and political challenges and successes that have occurred during recent work in sub-national forest degradation monitoring. The 2012 workshop, held in Bangkok, Thailand, followed recent US Forest Service/LEAF (USAID's Lowering Emissions in Asia's Forests) forest degradation monitoring options assessments that took place in Cambodia, Lao PDR and Viet Nam. Forest degradation can play a significant role in decreasing forest carbon, and therefore should be included in forest carbon monitoring for purposes of greenhouse gas inventories and participation in prospective carbon markets. Yet despite this, accurate monitoring methodologies are not widely available, and pertinent definitions and drivers are not clearly defined. The workshop allowed for a comprehensive update of techniques being used in case studies worldwide, in addition to the implications of forest degradation definitions and thresholds that lack consensus. Topics discussed included drivers at varying levels, remote sensing techniques and approaches, ground based field measurements, uncertainties and design considerations, integration of monitoring techniques, and regional themes and next steps.

Key words: forest degradation monitoring, Southeast Asia, climate change, carbon.

CIFOR	Center for International Forestry Research
DBH	diameter at breast height
FAO	Food and Agriculture Organization
FIPD	Forest Inventory and Planning Division
FRA 2015	Global Forest Resources Assessment 2015
GHG	Greenhouse Gas
GIS	Geographic Information Systems
GLAS	Geoscience Laser Altimeter System
GOFC GOLD	Global Observation of Forest and Land Cover Dynamics
GPS	Global Positioning System
IPCC	Intergovernmental Panel on Climate Change
I-REDD+	(the European Union's) Impacts of REDD+ project
IUCN	International Union for Conservation of Nature
LiDAR	Light Detection And Ranging
LEAF	Lowering Emissions in Asia's Forests
MODIS	Moderate Resolution Imaging Spectroradiometer
REDD+	Reducing Emissions from Deforestation and forest Degradation
RL	Reference Level
SNV	Netherlands Development Organization
SPOT 5	Systeme Pout l'Observation de la Terre Satellite
UNFCCC	United Nations Framework Convention on Climate Change
USAID/RDMA	United States Agency for International Development / Regional DevelopmentMission for A
USFS	United States Forest Service
USFS-IP	United States Forest Service-International Programs

Contents

Introduction

James Halperin[1] and David Ganz[2]

Globally, approximately two-thirds of the world's forests are considered degraded, but practical, cost-effective tools for monitoring forest quality remain elusive. Techniques for monitoring deforestation and changes to forest carbon stocks are widespread and well published. However, techniques for monitoring forest degradation are relatively untested in developing countries despite their inclusion in the United Nations Framework Convention on Climate Change (UNFCCC) negotiations on Reducing Emissions from Deforestation and Forest Degradation (REDD+). The lack of a forest degradation definition, challenges in forest monitoring methodologies, access to emerging technologies and knowledge, and the development of appropriate sampling frameworks all further complicate forest degradation monitoring.

The United States Agency for International Development/Regional Development Mission for Asia (USAID/RDMA)-funded Lowering Emissions in Asia's Forests (LEAF) program is designed to assist partner countries in Southeast Asia reduce negative impacts of unsustainable forest use on Greenhouse Gas (GHG) emissions. Two of LEAF's main objectives include building technical capacity for monitoring changes in forest carbon stocks and demonstrating innovation in sustainable land management. By collaborating directly with key departments and agencies in partner countries, LEAF aims to help its institutional partners reach their goals of reducing GHG emissions through improving both forest management and forest monitoring systems needed to reliably and transparently account for GHG emissions reductions in the forest sector.

LEAF is partnering with the United States Forest Service-International Programs (USFS-IP) to provide critical technical assistance in identifying and developing forest monitoring methodologies that can estimate GHG emissions, with a special emphasis on forest degradation. The key objectives of this partnership include:

- Assessing forest degradation drivers and monitoring options at the sub-national level in Lao PDR, Vietnam, and Cambodia;
- Convening a forest monitoring experts workshop to discuss lessons learned from the sub-national assessments and operational aspects of various forest degradation monitoring approaches, highlighting potentially successful approaches given existing drivers; and
- Communicating results of these activities to develop forest degradation monitoring demonstration programs and strengthen capacity in partner countries.

---

[1]Center for International Forestry Research, Lusaka, Zambia
[2]LEAF Asia, Liberty Square, Suite 2002, 287 Silom Road, Bangrak, Bangkok, 10500 Thailand
Corresponding author: j.halperin@cgiar.org

The goal of this proceedings document is to bring together the ideas and lessons learned from the forest monitoring experts' workshop. By exploring remote sensing tools, modeling, and field-based monitoring approaches, the workshop findings promote integrating feasible monitoring methods into national and sub-national forest monitoring systems, to detect how much degradation is taking place. Explicitly addressing degradation can reduce associated carbon emissions and protect largely intact forests before they suffer from degradation.

The experts who attended the forest monitoring experts' workshop represented a wide range of specialties and experience from national, regional, and global perspectives. Specific objectives of the workshop included both understanding implications of definitions in context of operationalizing forest monitoring degradation; and assessing case studies, and current and emerging best practices to detect and monitor forest degradation. Key questions from the workshop highlighted linkages between forest degradation drivers, monitoring methods and the challenges and opportunities associated with relevant monitoring methodologies.

The two-day workshop was formatted in order to take advantage of the range and depth of experience of the workshop participants. Morning presentations were followed by focus group discussions to thoroughly address questions such as:

- Which drivers and degradation sources can be detected;
- Which methods are most effective at detection and,
- What challenges and opportunities are involved in detecting degradation?

This proceedings report presents abstracts from presentations, followed by an in-depth analysis of conclusions from topic areas in remote sensing, ground based field measurements, uncertainty analysis, and integration of data sources. Key findings from the USFS sub-national assessments at LEAF intervention areas form a central component to link forest degradation drivers and monitoring options. This work thus builds upon country-level degradation assessments in Vietnam, Laos, and Cambodia, and is part of LEAF's commitment to building institutional technical capacity across the region for monitoring changes in forest carbon stocks and demonstrating innovations in sustainable land management. The focus group discussion summaries integrate combined knowledge from the participant experts with the lessons learned from the LEAF/USFS assessments in order to provide next steps for advancing forest degradation monitoring demonstration activities.

Forest degradation is a challenging concept to operationalize within forest monitoring programs. This holds true even in countries with long-standing forest monitoring experience. Spatial extent, occurrence, frequency, and intensity are all variables of forest degradation drivers that must be taken into account when developing forest degradation monitoring initiatives. LEAF and the US Forest Service hope that this document provides a solid base in addressing these issues to bring forest degradation monitoring into the mainstream.

Participants in the International Workshop on Monitoring Forest Degradation in Southeast Asia held November 13-14, 2012 in Bangkok, Thailand.
(Photo: Nicole Kravec)

Institutional Context, Drivers and Detectability in REDD+ Implementation

Village protection forest of Namat Village, Viengxay District, Lao PDR.
(Photo: James Halperin)

Section Summary

Patricia Manley[1]

REDD+ and Forest Degradation

REDD+ implementation requires two key steps: (1) establish a reference emission level or reference level (RL); and (2) monitor performance against the reference level (RL). A monitoring system must be able to monitor the performance of implementing action plans to reduce emissions. Degradation activities are of concern because it is unknown to what degree they are contributing to emissions, with potentially and in some cases likely significant contributions to emissions. For REDD+ the key feature is the need to estimate the net emissions from *anthropogenic-caused* (i.e., human-caused) changes in forests remaining forests.

Forest degradation is brought about by many factors, or drivers, resulting in different carbon impacts. International experts tend to agree that simple classifications are most useful, with two categories of drivers - direct (or proximate) and indirect (or underlying) – being commonly used (Kissinger et al. 2012). Direct forest degradation drivers are activities that cause long-term (persisting from some undefined number of years) loss in forest biomass, and directly contribute to CO_2 emissions. The duration of the impact in a given location can be a function of one or more activities, and a single event (pulse disturbance) or repeated use (chronic disturbance) over one or more decades.

Indirect drivers are the underlying causes that result in the occurrence of direct drivers. Currently there are no international agreements through IPCC or the UNFCCC on how to classify forest degradation drivers. However, relevant to a REDD+ mechanism, there are several ways to classify the activities that contribute to degradation of forests. International experts tend to agree that simple classifications are most easily understood. In this context, we adopted the direct and indirect drivers system recommended by Kissinger et al. 2012. Direct forest degradation drivers are human activities that cause a long-term loss in forest carbon stocks in forests that remain forests.

Characteristics of Degradation Activities

Degradation activities are dynamic across landscapes and over time. Individual activities are a function of the intersection of opportunity and need, and both of these factors are constantly changing in response to environmental and social pressures. Characteristics of individual activities include: occurrence (rare or common), spatial extent (limited or extensive), intensity (low or high impact per occurrence), temporal frequency (singular, recurring, chronic), and temporal persistence (short or extended recovery per occurrence).

---

[1]US Forest Service, Pacific Southwest Research Station, 2480 Carson Road, Placerville, CA 95667
Corresponding author: pmanley@fs.fed.us

Further, multiple degradation activities are often occurring in the same forested areas. A composite description of the spatial and temporal characteristics of individual degradation activities for a given landscape can provide a model for degradation across a given landscape. The model can then be studied to determine measurement approaches that are most effective and efficient. Similarly, available and proposed survey and monitoring designs can be evaluated relative to which degradation activities are expected to be detected and how reliably their impact may be captured. The characteristics of degradation activities across a given landscape (at any scale) can and will change in response to a variety of influences, including land use, resource use policies, and market forces. Characterizations and subsequent measurement and monitoring approaches need to be robust to changes in degradation activities over time.

Prevalent Direct Drivers

Current inventories of GHG emissions do not effectively account for degradation because associated emissions are difficult to detect. Manley et al. (this volume) conducted an assessment of degradation activities and monitoring options at the sub-national scale within three countries in Southeast Asia: Viet Nam, Lao PDR, and Cambodia. They found that six primary degradation activities were present in all districts, and common in one or more of them: planned selective tree harvest, unplanned selective tree harvest, commercial fuelwood collection, customary fuelwood collection, shifting cultivation, and wildfire. Tree harvest was widespread in all three assessments, whereas the other activities varied in their extent among the districts.

There are many challenges in defining, identifying, detecting, and quantifying losses or changes in carbon resulting from degradation. Some experts would argue that degradation is an inconsequential loss of carbon compared to deforestation and that it is too expensive and difficult to quantify. Others would argue that only those activities that result in substantial reductions in carbon density are worth pursuing, and they should be addressed individually. Yet others would argue that it is the degree of degradation in a given area that is of interest, not individual activities. Most would agree, however, that low levels of degradation – meaning minor losses in carbon density – are not the primary concern or target of degradation monitoring efforts. Workshop participants generally agreed that degradation was a significant source of carbon loss in many landscapes in Southeast Asia and neighboring countries, and that losses were likely to be substantial and needed to be quantified.

Degradation Detection and Estimation

A fundamental objective in any sampling effort is the ability to reliably detect the subject of the sampling effort. It may seem like an overly simplistic objective, but in reality many biological and physical features in natural environments are difficult to detect. Detectability is the ability for an observer to directly or indirectly determine the presence of the feature when it is present. Spatial distribution, extent, and intensity all affect the ability of a given sampling effort to detect carbon loss. For example, rare, small, or cryptic species may be difficult for observers to detect within a sample plot in the forest, even when they are present. In the case of degradation, if the degradation is low intensity (e.g., few small trees per hectare or small areas that are dispersed over a large landscape) it may be difficult to detect either by remote sensing (minimal reductions in canopy cover) or dispersed small (0.1 ha) sample plots. Landscape-wide data, such as remote sensing, provides a 100% sample, so detectability is a function of resolution of the imagery - high resolution will have greater detectability but is more expensive. Field-sampling methods that use larger plots and/or a high density of plots have a greater likelihood of detecting rare occurrences across a landscape, but variability in occurrence of degraded conditions greatly increases sample size requirements, thereby increasing the cost of field sampling.

Detection of degradation activities is also a function of temporal characteristics. If detectability is based on changes in canopy, it is likely to be highly ephemeral, or have a short half-life in that the effects quickly become difficult to detect while the impact is much longer lasting. For example, when a substantial proportion of the forest canopy is reduced through tree removal, gaps in the canopy are likely to recover quickly, but biomass will take much longer to recover. Multiple activities that occur on a periodic or chronic basis in the overlapping locations and varying over time present the most challenging scenario for detection and characterization of degradation, particularly detection of individual drivers.

Estimating Carbon Loss and Emissions

Fundamentally, there are two approaches to quantifying carbon losses and associated emissions: direct measure and estimation through statistical modeling. The stock-change method of accounting (compares two measurements of standing biomass taken at two or more points in time) relies more heavily on direct measure (although statistical modeling is still used to derive final estimates of emissions). The gain-loss method of accounting (comparison of gains derived through growth models and losses derived through estimation) requires information on the extent of degradation activities in order to model associated losses. In reality, reliable estimates can be used to enhance efficiency and accuracy in the use of either accounting method.

Planned activities, namely commercial timber harvest operations (particularly in areas that are not highly vulnerable to post-harvest unplanned tree removal), represent the most consistent and predictable degradation activity. As such, the ability to model and then estimate biomass reductions is greatest for planned timber harvest activities. For a given landscape (e.g., district or province), planned timber harvest may be consistent enough to develop emission factor estimates of reductions in biomass associated with standard silvicultural prescriptions implemented in certain forest types. This library of biomass losses can be generated through developing and refining estimates using remote sensing and field measurements for certain activities in certain forest types. With such a library of statistically modeled estimates, one would only need to know the forest type, the treatment prescription, and have medium resolution remote sensing data to estimate biomass reductions. This could be a very efficient means of estimating changes in carbon density and associated emissions; however, it is a reliable approach primarily where there is a high level of consistency in management activities.

The greatest extent of degradation activities arguably is unplanned degradation activities. These activities will have the greatest extent (occurring everywhere there is access) and they are likely to be highly variable over time and space in response to changing direct and indirect drivers, such as changes in local policies, subsidies, food availability and prices, and environmental quality. Thus, estimating changes in biomass and associated emissions is more challenging for this class of activities. It is possible for statistical estimation techniques to be used to either derive estimates or improve ground-based estimates of carbon loss. The risk of degradation may be more tractable to estimate than degradation intensity, with risk largely being a function of proximity, access, population density, and prosperity.

<u>Monitoring Challenges and Opportunities</u>

Clearly, no one monitoring approach will be most efficient and effective in all circumstances. Similarly, not all degradation activities can be, nor do they need to be, accounted for in a monitoring system. It seems most important to identify and achieve a given level of accuracy and precision in accounting for carbon loss and emissions, and to use whatever tools are available and effective in achieving that objective. In some cases, the greatest losses will be most reliably detected and characterized primarily by using direct field measurement. In other cases, high-resolution remote sensing data might be available and changes in biomass are readily estimates using these data. In most cases, however, it will be a combination of multiple sources of data that will provide the most reliable estimates over time.

The challenges include the following:
- Degradation activities and their characteristics can be highly variable across landscapes – particularly unplanned or customary activities associated with domestic uses of wood - and can change rapidly in their intensity in response to indirect drivers.
- The ecological consequences of forest carbon losses through degradation activities remains unexplored, but they are assumed to be a significant impact on forest quality.
- Given the complexity of human behavior, combined with variability in environmental factors acting on forested ecosystems, the challenge of monitoring changes in forest carbon becomes a socio-economic monitoring and modeling exercise, as much as it is an ecological one.
- Other than planned timber harvest activities, variability in degradation location and intensity makes it difficult to develop a standard set of emission factors associated with degradation even in a given location.
- Lower intensity degradation can be difficult to detect with remote sensing and difficult to quantify reliably using field data.
- Primary limitations of various data sources – moderate resolution remote sensing has low detectability, high resolution remote sensing comes at a higher cost and requires higher internal capacity, field-based data are only as reliable as trained field personnel and sample sizes afford - are likely to persist for 5-10 years into

the future, so we need to develop best practices and expectations based on available methods.

- Debate exists as to under what circumstances degradation is to be included in reference levels for REDD+.
  - o Needs to constitute a significant contribution to emissions, but how one defines significant is open.
  - o A degradation activity needs to be quantified to some degree before it can be determined to be significant.

The opportunities that lie ahead are the following:

- Broadly applicable tools can be developed that users can implement to estimate emissions associated with more standard, predictable activities, such as planned timber harvest.
- Decision support tools are also being developed that can be used to derive reference levels for REDD+, and decision support tools in general are becoming more readily available and user friendly
- High resolution remote sensing continues to become increasingly available and affordable, but fast-paced changes in technology impact its repeatability, which may make it most useful for training and validation as opposed to as a primary data source for carbon status or change.
- Small scale demonstration projects provide the opportunity to:
  1) Identify and validate the type and location of degradation activities that need to be quantified;
  2) Determine what detection and description methods best match the spatial and temporal characteristics of the primary degradation sources;
  3) Develop and refine modeling approaches that can maximize the efficiency of the monitoring system; and
  4) Demonstrate how to link these data in a decision support framework to develop robust reference levels and emission estimates.

Definitions in the Context of the United Nations Framework Convention on Climate Change

Sandra Brown[1]

Abstract

In relation to REDD+ implementation, two key steps are needed: (1) establishing a reference emission level or reference level (RL) and (2) monitoring performance against the RL. The RL is based on historic emissions and this can serve as a key starting point for designing any system for future monitoring. A monitoring system must be able to monitor the performance of implementing action plans to reduce emissions. Thus there is a need to know what actions are causing emissions. So designing a system for establishing the RL is the first step---need to know where, by which drivers, over what time frame, and the magnitude of the emissions for each driver. With regard to degradation, the IPCC provides a framework for accounting for such emissions--this is the change in carbon stocks of forests remaining forests. A common IPCC definition of forest degradation is: "A direct, human-induced, long-term loss (persisting for X years or more) of at least Y% of forest carbon stocks since time T and not qualifying as deforestation". Attempts are made to define the magnitude of X, Y and T, but I argue that this is not needed in detail—suffice it to say that for REDD+ the key feature is the need for estimating the net emissions from anthropogenic-caused (i.e. direct human caused) changes in forests remaining forests. Many drivers causing different carbon impacts bring about forest degradation, thus no one monitoring system will fit all causes. And the emissions for all causes of degradation may not need to be included in a monitoring system—it will depend on their magnitude relative to other emission sources. An overview of a decision support tool was presented that provides guidance on how to decide which degrading activities to include.

[1]Winrock International, 621 N Kent St., Suite 1200, Arlington, VA 22209
Corresponding author: SBrown@winrock.org

Degradation Activities, Drivers, and Emissions: US Forest Service LEAF Country Assessments

Patricia Manley[1], Leif Mortenson[2], James Halperin[3], and Rick Turner[4]

Abstract

Degradation is emerging as a common outcome of forest activities, and associated greenhouse gas (GHG) emissions have the potential to be significant. Understanding the activities and drivers of degradation is central to the ability to effectively measure, monitor, and mitigate associated emissions. Current inventories of GHG emissions do not effectively account for degradation because emissions are difficult to detect. We conducted an assessment of degradation activities and monitoring options at the sub-national scale within three countries in Southeast Asia: Viet Nam, Cambodia and Lao PDR. Visual surveys were conducted in the first half of 2012 across districts (Con Cuong, Aural, and Viengxay and Xamtai, respectively), which were ~200,000 ha in size. We found six primary degradation activities that were present in all districts, and common in one or more of them: planned selective tree harvest, unplanned selective tree harvest, commercial fuelwood collection, customary fuelwood collection, shifting cultivation, and wildfire. Timber harvest was widespread in all three assessments, whereas the other activities varied in their extent among the districts. Shifting cultivation was quite commonly occurring in Lao PDR, wildfire was a concern in all districts, but was prevalent in Cambodia. Fuelwood collection occurred in all districts, but was widespread and intensive in some locations in Viet Nam. The character of degradation activities affects their ability to be adequately measured and monitored with available methods. Characteristics affecting the ability of measurement methods to detect and adequately describe (i.e., accuracy and precision) include: occurrence (rare or common), spatial extent (limited or extensive), intensity (low or high impact), and temporal persistence (shifting, recurring, or chronic). A composite description of the spatial and temporal characteristics of individual degradation activities for a given landscape provides a blueprint for designing measurement approaches that are effective and efficient. Similarly, proposed survey and monitoring designs can be evaluated relative to which degradation activities are expected to be detected and how well their impact will be captured. The characteristics of degradation activities across a given landscape (at any scale) can and will change in response to a variety of influences, including land use, resource use policies, and market forces. Characterizations and subsequent measurement and monitoring approaches need to be robust to changes in degradation activities over time.

---

[1] US Forest Service, Pacific Southwest Research Station, 2480 Carson Road, Placerville, CA 95667
[2] US Forest Service, Pacific Northwest Research Station, 620 SW Main St. Suite 400, Portland, OR 97205
[3] Center for International Forestry Research, Lusaka, Zambia
[4] US Forest Service, Tongass National Forest, 8510 Mendenhall Loop Road, Juneau AK, 99801
Corresponding author: pmanley@fs.fed.us

Remote Sensing

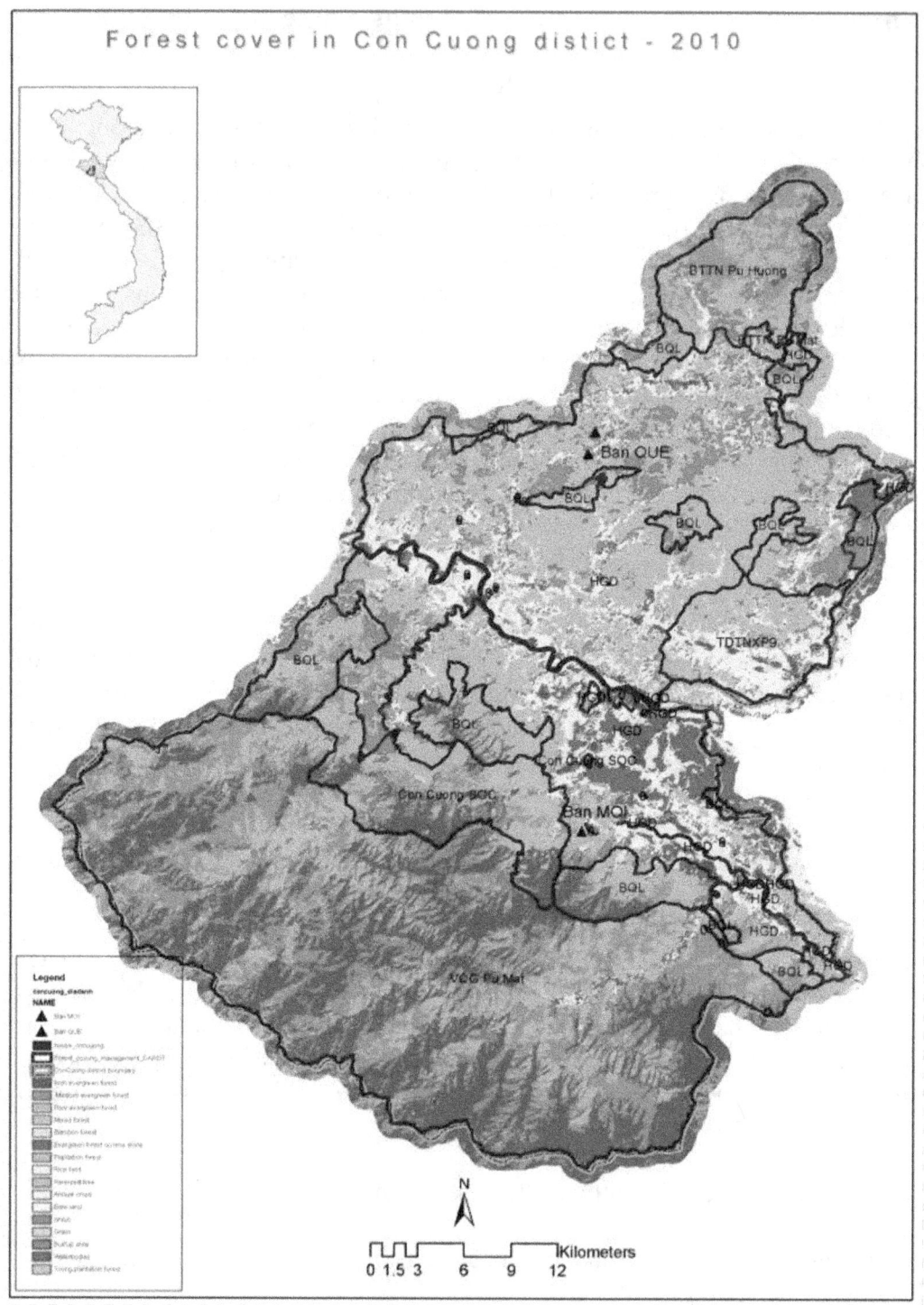

2010 Land cover map of Con Cuong District, Nghe An Province, north-central Viet Nam.
(Map produced by LEAF/SNV-Viet Nam, 2012)

Section Summary

Belinda Arunarwati Margono[1,2]

Remote sensing is an important data source for monitoring the change of forest cover, in terms of both total removal of forest cover (deforestation), and change of canopy cover, structure and forest ecosystem services that result in forest degradation. In the context of Intergovernmental Panel on Climate Change (IPCC), forest degradation monitoring requires information regarding the degree of forest disturbance that results in a reduction in carbon stock within a specific time interval. Currently, remote sensing data does not directly provide readily available information on how much carbon has been released from a disturbed forest. In this regard, the integration between remote sensing data and field/ground based measurement is key. While many types of remote sensing can detect total loss of forest cover (deforestation), it is more challenging but still feasible for remote sensing data to detect changes in the extent of remaining forests that have been disturbed. Advanced techniques for analyzing remote sensing data are able to roughly estimate the area of disturbance; however it should be equipped with sufficient field verification. Field data is needed to provide estimates about how much biomass or carbon has been removed per unit area of the disturbance.

An agreement on the main direct drivers of forest degradation is of vital need for use of remote sensing data. Consensus on the main direct drivers will lead to a general understanding of the scale and intensity of disturbances that can be detected by the selected remote sensing data. In general, forest degradation is the effect of forest logging activities, either selective planned logging or illegal logging. Currently, remote sensing can detect forest degradation through indicators such as canopy disturbance and infrastructure development (forest roads, logging roads logging decks, etc.). However, the ability of remote sensing data to detect the above indicators depends on the spatial and spectral resolution. Higher resolution data (e.g., LiDAR) provides more detailed information but also has higher costs for data acquisition, data processing, and data management. Lower resolution data (e.g., Landsat) provides a less sensitive measure of forest change, but is more readily obtained and repeated. The availability and repeatability of remote sensing data has implications in the tropics for obtaining cloud-free images and detecting, degradation with rapid post-disturbance canopy recovery. These strengths and weaknesses should be taken into consideration to select appropriate remote sensing data for the application.

Setting the objectives of monitoring is a key for setting an efficient system; and a general understanding of forest degradation drivers will assist in determining these objectives. Once monitoring objectives are determined, it is possible to assess monitoring options based on desired precision and financial considerations. In terms of financial considerations, very high spatial and spectral remote sensing data combined with

[1]Department of Geographical Sciences, University of Maryland, College Park, MD 20742
[2]Ministry of Forestry of Indonesia, Jakarta 10270, Indonesia
Corresponding author: bmargono@umd.edu

advanced processing techniques should only be introduced for specific areas of interest and may not be favorable for wall to wall mapping at a national scale. Further, the availability of required hardware, software and capacity human resources are also important considerations.

Main challenges

General challenges of using remote sensing data for monitoring forest degradation in the tropics:
- Persistent clouds and haze in tropical areas lead to difficulties in acquiring cloud-free remote sensing data needed to fulfill monitoring objectives.
- Data continuity is a big challenge in establishing a credible forest resource monitoring system. A sufficient monitoring system must be supported by the use of remote sensing data that ensure data continuity and availability.
- Data analysis repeatability is another consideration. The techniques for analyzing the data must be implementable, replicable and must allow for the use of alternative data instead of selected remote sensing data when necessary.
- Steep terrain and forest seasonality in certain areas require specific methodologies (e.g., more image processing procedures and more field verification).
- Determining at what point high-resolution remote sensing data sets and advanced techniques need to be applied, and how to link those results with wall-to-wall interpreted maps derived from lower resolution data sources.
- A comprehensive package of human resource technical requirements, hardware and software is very important for developing a credible monitoring system, thus continued capacity building/strengthening are required to get optimal results.

More specific challenges:
- Clearly defining the causes of forest degradation in the area of interest is paramount. Lack of understanding about the local causes of forest degradation can result in activities that may not contribute to the monitoring objective.
- Dynamic change of forest cover as a result of fast crown recovery after disturbance in the tropics is another key issue. Appropriate spatio-temporal data sets need to be used to capture dynamic forest cover changes.
- Complex forest structure and composition in tropical forests are sometimes difficult to analyze with remote sensing data; for example vegetation indices, such as Leaf Area Index, will saturate after a value of 4-6 m^2/m^2 in tropical forests.
- Mismatched time of data acquisition and field data collection is a classic problem, especially in developing countries where budgets for field surveys are often inadequate. It is important to complete and process ground based field measurements that temporally coincide with remotely sensed data acquisition. Mismatches in time between the field measurements and remote sensing data sets lead to errors in analysis.
- Ability to detect single/individual tree removal by selective logging is another key issue, and likely requires high spatial resolution data. For this, there is a need to obtain imagery that is spatially and spectrally able to detect individual tree crowns, and temporally close in time to the logging activity.

14

Promising opportunities/approaches

- Roughly define the main driver(s) of forest degradation in the area of interest and select appropriate indicators that can be used for deriving information from remote sensing data (e.g., change in canopy cover).
- In general, select basic/simple classes for forest extent (e.g. dividing area of 'forest remaining forest') into two main classes, such as primary undisturbed forest and degraded forest. Segregating different degrees of degradation can be accomplished when appropriate high-resolution spatial data and sufficient field validation are available.
- Develop and apply a low cost policy to provide high spatial resolution data set, including simple procedures for data pre-processing.
- Develop and apply methods using high spatial resolution data and advanced techniques (e.g. the method applied for Guyana) for analyzing a specific area of interest. This is necessary to test the method (or other possible methods) in different areas, especially areas with steep terrain and deciduous forest types.
- Apply timely field/ground data measurement in order to support forest inventory programs and validate remote sensing results. The field measurements should focus on providing information on forest disturbance and potential carbon released.
- Hybrid approach of using a per-pixel classification method and a GIS-based fragmentation method to map degraded forest (e.g. the method applied for Sumatera-Indonesia) can be applied to developing national wall-to-wall coverages.

Detecting and Monitoring Deforestation and Forest Degradation: Issues and Obstacles for Southeast Asia

Douglas Muchoney[1] and Sharon Hamann[1]

Abstract

Forest degradation can be defined as the loss of forest volume, biomass and/or forest productivity caused by natural or human influences. Achieving Reduced Emissions from Deforestation and Forest Degradation (REDD+) requires that deforestation and degradation can be efficiently, reliably, and cost-effectively detected and quantified, often where ground and aerial surveying is problematic. Therefore, remote sensing approaches, coupled with field and/or aerial data, offer possible solutions and efficiencies. While synoptic coverage using high-resolution data such as Landsat can provide estimates of deforestation and degradation, very high-resolution satellite data can be used to calibrate and validate these estimates in a multi-stage sampling approach. This research coupled Landsat and very high-resolution satellite optical data to determine whether Landsat could quantify deforestation and degradation in montane and lowland forests of Cambodia. Initial results are that Landsat can detect deforestation, and also the "halo" effect of degradation from high-grading in areas adjacent to deforested areas. Issues include high-resolution data that have different spatial, temporal and radiometric characteristics, and were not necessarily acquired at the same time as the Landsat data. The ability to detect deforestation and degradation is also a function of when an event is imaged the level and type of disturbance/degradation, and the type and age of the forest.

[1]U.S. Geological Survey, Climate and Land-Use Change, 519 National Center, Reston, VA 20192 USA
Corresponding author: dmuchoney@usgs.gov

Measuring Global Canopy Reduction: A Forest Degradation Proxy for FRA2015

Kenneth MacDicken[1] and Erik Lindquist[1]

Abstract

Global interest in forest degradation is widespread – but is fraught with widely differing views. Forest degradation by one definition may be sustainable forest management by another. The Global Forest Resources Assessment, conducted by FAO every five years, is working to find an approach to a global estimation of forest area that can address these differing views. This approach is based on the use of MODIS VCS satellite data to evaluate significant forest canopy reduction over a ten year time span. Significance in this case will be calculated as a threshold (most likely 20%) reduction in canopy area at the pixel scale. The reduction in forest canopy area may or may not be seen as degradation – depending on the values of the data user.

This analysis will be completed during 2013 for use in FRA 2015 and will provide summaries of reduced forest area globally, regionally and by ecological zone. Country representatives will be provided with data from the initial analysis done by FAO so that they can review and revise as needed. A tier system will be used as part of FRA 2015 to describe the overall level of each variable – including the reduced forest canopy area. While not a report of forest degradation directly, it is intended to be a proxy that can provide at least some indication of the area of forest in which human activities have resulted in reduced canopy density forest.

[1]FAO Forest Resources Assessment, Vialedelle Terme di Caracalla 15, 00100 Rome, Italy
Corresponding author: Kenneth.MacDicken@fao.org

Remote Sensing Application Challenges
in the Mekong Region

Jeffrey Himel[1]

Abstract

Forest degradation is not just one of the cornerstones of "REDD+", it is a critical element for Lao PDR and other countries where the primary driver of forest carbon loss is selective logging and small-scale conversion of forest for agriculture rather than deforestation. Unless we can reliably and accurately quantify the area of degradation using remote sensing technology, REDD+ will not be viable. This is complicated by the need to separate degradation from other changes within forests that have effects similar to degradation, such as seasonal change in deciduous trees (e.g., dropping leaves).
Lao PDR has developed a good quality data and experience base through the efforts of the Forest Inventory and Planning Division (FIPD) with the support of a range of coordinated donors. FIPD has acquired and processed wall-to-wall satellite imagery covering Lao PDR for 1995 and 2000 using LandSAT, 2005 using SPOT 5 and 2010 using RapidEye. FIPD analysts are finalizing the Benchmark and Historical Forest Cover Maps for these time periods. Lessons learned through this work highlight the importance of *first principles*: image pre-processing, image analysis, and accuracy assessment. Investment in careful and quality pre-processing of 5to 10m-resolution satellite imagery like RapidEye provides the best "bang for the buck". This pre-processing includes ortho-rectification to 1:25,000 scale, and proper haze removal. Object-based image processing provides an excellent starting point for analysis, from which we can work backwards and train staff to become more consistent and progressively improve the accuracy of their work. Full annual or semi-annual country coverage at 5m is now feasible technically and cost-wise and so should be a top priority for donors. Wall-to-wall RapidEye coverage of Lao PDR for 2010 cost a total of US$225,000.

[1]Aruna Technology Ltd, 417 Sisowath Blvd., Sangkat Chaktomuk, Phnom Penh, Cambodia
Corresponding author: jeffrey.himel@arunatechnology.com

Assessing Forest Degradation in Guyana with GeoEye, Quickbird and Landsat

Bobby Braswell[1], Steve Hagen[1], William Salas[1], Michael Palace[2], Sandra Brown[3], Felipe Casarim[3], and Nancy Harris[3]

Abstract

Forest degradation is defined as a change in forest quality and condition (e.g. reduction in biomass), while deforestation is a change in forest area. This pilot study evaluated several image processing approaches to map degradation and estimate carbon removals from logging. From the Joint Concept Note on REDD+ cooperation between Guyana and Norway carbon loss as indirect effect of new infrastructure is addressed as follows: "The establishment of new infrastructure in forest areas often contributes to forest carbon loss outside the areas directly affected by construction. Unless a larger or smaller area or greenhouse gas emission impact can be documented through remote sensing or field observations, the area within a distance extending 500 meters from the new infrastructure (incl. mining sites, roads, pipelines, reservoirs) shall be accounted with a 50% annual carbon loss through forest degradation." Our premise is that if we can detect logging at various levels of intensity equivalent to less than 50% removal, then we can apply this approach to examine degradation surrounding new infrastructure. For this preliminary degradation analysis, we examined two Landsat 5 TM images and two high-resolution scenes from GeoEye/Quickbird from central Guyana. Field data on logging concession (maximum allowable cut) and logging impacts of forest gaps were used to test a suite of image processing approaches. Our goal was to examine areas known to be recently logged (i.e. degraded) and quantify the signal in the remote sensing data from this activity. From this analysis, we present results comparing pre-logging imagery to imagery acquired approximately post-logging.

[1]Applied Geosolutions, 87 Packers Falls Rd., Durham, NH 03924
[2]Institute for the Study of Earth, Oceans and Space, Complex System Research Center, Morse Hall, University of New Hampshire, 39 College Road, Durham, NH 03824
[3]Winrock International, 621 N Kent St., Suite 1200, Arlington, VA 22209
Corresponding author: wsalas@appliedgeosolutions.com

Mapping Deforestation and Forest Degradation Using Landsat Time Series: a Case of Sumatra—Indonesia

Belinda Arunarwati Margono[1, 2]

Abstract

Indonesia experiences the second highest rate of deforestation among tropical countries (FAO 2005, 2010). Consequently, timely and accurate forest data are required to combat deforestation and forest degradation in support of climate change mitigation and biodiversity conservation policy initiatives. Remote sensing is considered as a significant data source for forest monitoring purposes, and has been widely used for monitoring deforestation and forest degradation. However, varying definitions have been an obstacle for optimizing the use of remote sensing for a reliable monitoring system, in addition to the problem of cloud cover in Indonesia. In this work, we demonstrate an applicable definition and methods that enable using remote sensing data sets for forest monitoring. We examined Sumatra as a case study, as Sumatra Island stands out due to intensive forest clearing that has resulted in the conversion of 70% of the island's forested area through 2010. We present here a hybrid approach to quantifying the extent and change of primary forest in terms of primary intact and primary degraded classes using per-pixel supervised classification mapping followed by a GIS-based fragmentation analysis. Loss of Sumatra's primary intact and primary degraded forests was estimated to provide suitable information for the objectives of the United Nations Framework on Climate Change (UNFCCC) and the Reducing Emissions from Deforestation and Forest Degradation (REDD and REDD+) program. Results quantified 7.54Mha of primary forest loss in Sumatra during the last two decades (1990-2010). An additional 2.31Mha of primary forest was degraded. Of the 7.54Mha cleared, 7.25Mha was in a degraded state when cleared, and 0.28Mha was in a primary state. The Geoscience Laser Altimeter System (GLAS) data set was employed to evaluate results. GLAS-derived tree canopy height indicated a significant structural difference between primary intact and primary degraded forests (mean height 28m $\pm$ 8.7m and 19m $\pm$ 8.2m, respectively). Results demonstrate a method for quantifying primary forest cover stand-replacement disturbance and degradation that can be replicated across the tropics in support of REDD+ initiatives. Furthermore, we can incorporate the results with the biomass assessment derived from GLAS data to illustrate the biomass by type in Sumatra.

[1]Department of Geographical Sciences, University of Maryland, College Park, MD 20742
[2]Ministry of Forestry of Indonesia, Jakarta 10270, Indonesia
Corresponding author: bmargono@umd.edu

Ground-Based Field Measurements

Outlining the location of plots along L-shaped transects in Long Kem village cluster, Xamtai District, Houaphanh Province, Lao PDR. (Photo: Leif Mortenson)

Section Summary

Nophea Sasaki[1]

Although deforestation has been the main focus of international debate in REDD+, forest degradation could emit even more carbon emissions because forest degradation can take place in any accessible forest. Accounting for emission factors requires the use of stock-change or gain-loss approach depending on the forests in questions. Ground based field measurements are a critical basis for both approaches. Carbon stocks in logged forests could vary highly depending to some extent on logging intensity and collateral damages.

Obtaining area estimates, or activity data, of degraded forest requires remote sensing but without clear definition of "forest degradation", it may not be possible using traditional remote sensing. Change detection techniques, along with information on logging planning and operations, become important to derive the activity data. The challenge is that information on degraded forest caused by unplanned logging is difficult to obtain because such logging is not easy to detect at a landscape or regional scale. At local scales, for example in a REDD+ project site, unplanned logging could however be tracked.

Monitoring forest degradation, and related carbon emissions and biodiversity loss, requires understanding of how trees were selectively harvested. Experience in tropical forest management suggests that in many instances, forest degradation is caused by unsustainable felling of commercially valuable timber species for immediate profits. This was found to be true in northeastern Cambodia, which was documented in a case study by Sasaki et al. (this volume).

- Unplanned selective logging for timber is a major driver of forest degradation as commercially valuable timber species are likely to be harvested. For example, in Southeast Asia highly expensive timber from trees such as *Dalbergia cochinchinensis* can be sold by the kilogram. In this case, any individuals with a chainsaw can fell trees and transport their timber for sale, even without a road network. Unplanned logging makes it difficult to monitor the degradation because location of the felled trees is not known.

- With planned selective logging, often all marketable trees (i.e., with diameter greater than 30 cm) are harvested. The harvested area is still forest by current definitions but between 40 and 50% of pre-harvest carbon stocks (Sasaki et al. this volume) could be lost. Resulting net carbon emissions will depend on the intensity of extraction methods, post harvest wood residue, post harvest growth rates, and amount of carbon in harvested wood products.

- Monitoring forest degradation at landscape or regional scale with affordable costs needs tools and resources that can relate forest canopy loss to biomass loss from individual trees or, more likely, a group of tree species according to their plant functional types with remote sensing technology. There is a strong need for improved allometric relationships to relate forest canopy parameters to biomass.

---

[1] United Graduate School of Applied Informatics, Harborland Center Building 22F, 1-3-3 Hiagashikawasaki-cho, Chuo-ku, Kobe, 650-0044, Japan
Corresponding author: nopsasaki@gmail.com

Financing incentives require political commitment from developing countries and all logging companies should have a minimum number of certified foresters to carry out logging planning and operations. With the aid of GPS and GIS technology, a transparent platform for tracking local activities could help monitor forest degradation.

Full accounting for carbon emissions from tropical forest degradation needs an understanding of two important variables, namely the activity data and emission factors relevant to the forests in question. As an example, Winrock International has proposed two methods for estimating net carbon emissions for forest harvesting practices in Guyana.

- Method 1: a standard approach of using medium resolution imagery to monitor the expansion of logging infrastructure into non-logged areas to obtain activity data combined with ground plots and the stock-change method for emission factors. Emission factors are the difference between C of unlogged and logged forests. However, the condition of logged forests is likely to be highly variable depending on forest type, logging intensity, location, growth rate, and the post-harvesting human activities. These conditions will increase uncertainty of pre- and post-harvest carbon stock estimates.

- Method 2: a combination of data sources such as timber extraction rates, management plans, and very high-resolution imagery for activity data combined with ground measurements in active logging gaps/concessions and the gain-loss method for emission factors. Estimating logging gaps in active timber concessions could be done using change detection technique and the loss in live biomass caused all harvesting activities, such as felling, damage to the residual stand, and creation of skid trails, log landings, and roads are then linked to the unit of timber removed (e.g. cubic meters).

- The carbon stock emissions from skid trail creation can be obtained from ground measurements by mapping and measuring the area of a sample of skid rails using GPS and measuring the damaged trees along the trails—such data can be linked to timber extraction rates.

Costs are another concern in forest carbon monitoring. The European Union's project on the Impacts of Reducing Emissions from Deforestation and Forest Degradation and Enhancing Carbon Stocks (I-REDD+) work package 4 focuses on community based monitoring. Community based monitoring offers great potential for lowering costs while providing direct tree measurement. Direct tree measurements on the ground are necessary as part of the ground truthing activities to check the correctness of the remote sensing based activity data. Direct tree measurements are also paramount for developing biomass estimates in either stock-change or gain-loss methodologies.

- I-REDD+'s study sought to evaluate the accuracy and cost effectiveness of monitoring performed by local communities versus professional foresters in four study sites in China, Vietnam, Indonesia and Laos. Community members were trained in establishing sample plots, measuring trees and using simple field protocols.

- A total of 289 sample plots were established between 2011 and 2012 and both local communities and professional foresters were involved in measuring trees in all these plots. Comparison of the carbon stock estimates between the two groups show that there was no significant difference except in forest types with very high biomass. Although the initial costs of training community members were high, community's involvement in forest monitoring can significantly reduce the costs on salaries, transportation, accommodation and other costs compared to that when professional foresters were hired.

- In addition, the involvement of communities in monitoring can directly be linked to effective benefit sharing from REDD+ and improvement of forest governance. Accordingly, if carbon stocks are measured locally, communities are likely to put more efforts on managing their forested areas for carbon and biodiversity conservation.

Main challenges and opportunities

- Monitoring forest degradation requires the development of a tool that can relate the loss of canopy cover of individual trees or group of individual trees to carbon stocks. By so doing, one can monitor carbon and biodiversity loss at the landscape or regional scale.

- Unmanaged harvesting for fuel wood and charcoal production is very difficult to monitor with precision. Tree stump surveys are one way to detect these activities and estimate associated carbon stock losses.

- In managed areas, it is possible to use a stock-change approach. However, even with proper stratification by year of harvest and extraction rate, intensive sampling may be needed to obtain reasonable precision of carbon emission estimates. Intensive fieldwork is also needed to establish the models for loss-gain approaches. Although once the models are established they can be used cost-effectively.

- Accounting for carbon storage in harvested wood products needs a life cycle assessment of the products in questions. This is necessary because carbon emissions from wood products depend very much on turnover rates and these rates depend on how the products are used.

- Accounting for carbon in post-harvest wood residue will require post-harvest surveys to estimate the 'dead wood' carbon pool, as well as knowledge of decay rates. Otherwise, wood residue could be considered a "committed emission".

- Carbon removals during regrowth after logging (i.e., sequestration) need to be accounted for to estimate net emissions. Removals can be estimated by collecting data in a chronosequence of logging gaps. Accurate information on site history will be needed along with repeated measurements of permanent sample plots.

- Involvement of local people (communities) in forest monitoring activities could achieve significant cost reduction while increasing the sense of responsibility of local people for protecting their forests for carbon and related benefits.

Carbon and Biodiversity Loss Due to Forest Degradation – a Cambodian Case Study

Nophea Sasaki[1], Kimsun Chheng[2], and Nobuya Mizoue[3]

Abstract

Tropical forests are diverse in terms of stand and age structures, commercial and biodiversity values of individually trees, and dependency of local communities. Monitoring forest degradation in the tropics remains a challenge despite increasing global interests in reducing carbon emissions from deforestation and forest degradation and safeguarding biodiversity and local benefits. Monitoring forest degradation and related carbon emissions require understanding of selective logging practice and its decision in felling the trees. Based on data from 179 sample plots across three provinces in Cambodia, this study discussed the process of forest degradation and related carbon emissions in selectively logged forests. Data were analyzed for forest health quality and timber grades according to DBH size class (10-19, 20-29, 30-39, 40-49, 50-59, and 60+ cm), as timber harvesting under unplanned logging is typically based on these variables.

Mean tree density and aboveground carbon stocks were estimated at 334.3 trees/ha and 360.2 $MgCO^2$/ha, respectively. In terms of carbon stocks, 36.8%, 44.9%, and 18.3% are respectively in forest health quality A, B, and C, suggesting forest condition is still good. Large trees in quality A and B are likely to be harvested as they have high commercial values. If all large trees (DBH>40 cm) are harvested, 45.6% of carbon stocks are gone and will gradually emit CO^2 depending on how the harvested wood is used. Carbon in branches, wood wastes onsite and offsite will be released immediately. Timber grades will also influence the decision making of the loggers because of the prices. Trees in luxury grade are more expensive and most of those tree species are classified as critically endangered by the IUCN. Despite progress in remote sensing technology, monitoring the loss of such valuable trees remains a challenge unless methods to link canopy cover with individual tree species are developed, and the relevant users are trained.

[1] United Graduate School of Applied Informatics, Harborland Center Building 22F, 1-3-3 Hiagashikawasaki-cho, Chuo-ku, Kobe, 650-0044, Japan
[2] Forestry Administration, #40 PreahNorodom Blvd., Phsar Kandal 2, Khann Daun Penh, Phnom Penh, Cambodia
[3] Laboratory of Forest Planning, Faculty of Agriculture, Kyushu University, Fukuoka 812-8581, Japan
Corresponding author: nopsasaki@gmail.com

Local Involvement in Measuring and Governing Carbon Stocks in China, Vietnam, Indonesia and Laos

Michael Køie Poulsen[1]

Abstract

An important element of MRV is to ensure accurate measurements of carbon stocks. Measuring trees on the ground may be needed for ground truthing of remote sensing results. It can also provide more accurate carbon stock monitoring than remote sensing alone. Local involvement in measuring trees for monitoring of carbon stocks may be advantageous in several ways. Involving local communities in monitoring of biomass in REDD+ schemes may cut costs of ground truthing and data gathering on changing rates of forest degradation. Moreover, local involvement can encourage local ownership of REDD+ projects. Empowering communities to monitor forest biomass carbon stocks may also contribute to local livelihoods and forest biodiversity conservation.

But how well does community-based monitoring compare with monitoring by professional foresters? Work Package 4 under the EU I-REDD+ project is examining monitoring of forest biomass executed by local communities and professional foresters and is evaluating the accuracy and cost-effectiveness of monitoring with local participation.

Local community members in four I-REDD+ study sites in China, Vietnam, Indonesia and Laos have been trained in establishing vegetation plots, measuring trees and using simple field protocols. Community members participated in the establishment of 289 vegetation plots. During 2011 and 2012, the level of forest carbon was measured by both local communities and professional foresters in all these plots. The estimated levels of carbon were essentially the same whether community members or professional foresters did the work. Thus, there should be no scientific obstacles to involving communities. This will also reduce transaction costs over time compared to having professional foresters undertake all the measurements. The initial costs of training community members may be high, but more can be saved over time on salaries, transportation, accommodation and other costs for professional foresters.

The involvement of communities in monitoring is directly linked to how benefits from REDD+ are distributed. Where control rights are shared between government and local communities, Benefit Distribution Mechanisms will be more just than when natural forests are under top-down state governance. Communities who can see the connection between correct measurement of carbon and the benefits received are most likely to manage their forested areas appropriately for carbon conservation. Forests managed for carbon conservation are also likely to preserve forest biodiversity.

The I-REDD+ project will continue its work in China, Indonesia, Lao PDR and Vietnam from 2011 to 2014.

[1]Skindergade 23, 1159 Copenhagen K, Denmark
Corresponding author: mkp@nordeco.dk

Methods for Monitoring Emissions and Removals from Forest Harvesting for Timber and Fuelwood: Lessons from Guyana

Sandra Brown[1]

Abstract

Two methodologies for estimating net emissions from forest harvesting practices (for timber and possibly fuel) are presented: (1) a standard approach of using medium resolution imagery to monitor the expansion of logging infrastructure into non-logged areas for activity data combined with ground plots and the stock-change method for emission factors; and (2) a combination of data sources (timber extraction rates, management plans, very high resolution imagery) for activity data combined with ground measurements in active logging gaps/concessions and the gain-loss method for emission factors. For methodology 1, the carbon stock of logged forests is likely to be extremely variable and it will likely be difficult to meet a reasonable precision level without stratification by year of harvest and timber extraction rates and by intensive ground sampling using plots. Although logging roads and log landings can be identified and their area obtained from the medium resolution imagery, skid trails, which also cause damage and emissions, cannot be unambiguously identified in the imagery. For methodology 2, the emissions are estimated directly in the gaps, using the concept of change detection, in active timber concessions—the loss in live biomass is caused by felling the trees and the collateral damage caused as the tree falls and the emissions are then linked to the unit of timber removed (e.g. cubic meters). The emissions from skid trails can be obtained from ground measurements by mapping and measuring the area of a sample of skid rails using GPS and measuring the damaged trees along the trails—such data can be linked to timber extraction rates. The emissions from infrastructure such as roads and landings can be obtained in a manner similar to methodology 1. Carbon removals during regrowth after logging (the gains) can be estimated by collecting data in a chronosequence of logging gaps. The steps described for methodology 2 were implemented for the period 2001 to 2010 in Guyana as a case study, and the results for the net annual emissions from timber extraction, including an uncertainty analysis, are presented.

---

[1]Winrock International, 621 N Kent St., Suite 1200, Arlington, VA 22209
Corresponding author: SBrown@winrock.org

Uncertainty and Design Considerations

Deciduous forest in the eastern area of Central Cardamom Protected Forest, Cambodia.
(Photo: James Halperin)

Section Summary

Stephen Hagen[1]

Well planned sampling designs and robust approaches to estimating uncertainty are critical components of forest monitoring. The importance of uncertainty estimation increases as deforestation and degradation issues become more closely tied to financing incentives for reducing greenhouse gas emissions in the forest sector. Investors like to know risk and risk is tightly linked to uncertainty. Uncertainty assessment is also important for evaluating the implications of forest management actions, and it helps us identify and design future projects to reduce uncertainty.

Design considerations

The conservative principle for accountable carbon credits allows credit for the estimated lower 95% confidence limit of carbon stock resulting from the project minus the expected baseline carbon stock. This serves as a financial incentive to reduce uncertainties where possible. Uncertainties in forest stock carbon estimates can be reduced by a) inventory planning and sampling design optimization; b) technological development; and c) biomass allometric models.

A rational decision about an optimal design can be made only by comparing the set of alternatives using objective selection criteria that combine information on survey cost and the achievable reliability of the results. Many choices exist for optimizing sampling design. For example, the selection of plot locations can be chosen by systematic sampling, simple random sampling or stratified random sampling. The optimal plot design depends on objectives, costs, and variability of the population's attributes of interest. Inventory planning steps include 1) identifying information needs and priorities; 2) assembling and evaluating existing data to answer the questions; 3) selecting the main monitoring components; and 4) setting the precision and cost requirements to compute the optimal sample size. During optimization, one should minimize the total inventory cost subject to fixed precision requirements (confidence interval and confidence level) for key attributes of interest. After this process, the objectives and priorities should be reevaluated and the process should be repeated.

There are many technological approaches that can help reduce error and increase confidence. Some examples include, a) improving the link between remote sensing and ground sampling; b) matching the imagery pixel resolution with the field plot size; c) improving the temporal resolution of remote sensing data; and d) reducing locational error by using survey-grade GPS to improve the links between remote sensing imagery and ground sampling (but with increased cost). In terms of statistical methods, several

[1]Applied Geosolutions, 87 Packers Falls Rd., Durham, NH 03924
Corresponding author: shagen@appliedgeosolutions.com

technological developments are potentially useful including a) using regression to link modeled imagery to plots; b) using double sampling for stratification or regression; c) using stratification to create homogenous strata with respect to key attributes and costs; d) allocating plots to strata based on stratum size, variance, and/or costs; and e) making all plots permanent initially, but remeasuring based on change strata.

Improvements to biomass allometric models may include a) developing regional models to help cover the range of species, growth forms, and wood densities; b) including large trees and buttressed trees in equations; c) using Randomized Branch Sampling on a subsample of trees as a means to correct for bias in the biomass models; and d) terrestrial laser scanning for individual stem volume (which shows promise, but may be challenging to apply in the tropics).

Uncertainty

Approaches for quantifying uncertainty should be decided upon at the initiation of a project. Unfortunately, this is typically done, if at all, at the end of a project; after the final products have been created.

Uncertainties are a composite of errors arising from observations and models. Different types of errors can be quantified by their precision, accuracy, or bias. Precision is the variation about the sample mean. Accuracy is the variation about the true mean, which includes both precision and bias. Bias occurs when the sample mean differs systematically from the true mean. Uncertainties can arise from multiple sources. For instance, we will never know the true values of large forest population parameters, so we measure a subsample of all of the individuals. The inaccuracy of estimation of these parameters from sample results is termed the sampling error. The size of sampling errors can be controlled by the survey design and the size of the sample. Non-sampling errors come from all other sources, such as faulty application of definitions, classification errors, measurement errors, model application errors, calculation errors, and sampling frame errors. These errors must be addressed on a case-by-case basis, through training and other quality control measures. To calculate the error budgets of total survey error, one needs to systematically identify and define all potential sources of error, Assess importance of each error and develop cost functions for reducing them, and balance the risk of mistakes due to the uncertainties with the cost of reducing the magnitude of the uncertainties.

The most common approach to combining uncertainties from multiple sources is to "sum by quadrature". In this approach, given uncertainties from multiple sources, total uncertainty is calculated as the square root of the sum of the squared uncertainty from all individual sources. This approach requires assumptions about the data, such as having a normal distribution, that are often incorrect.

A Monte Carlo framework with bootstrapping allows one to combine uncertainties from many sources and does not require assumptions about data distributions. It provides a means of handling non-linear models and data with complicating characteristics such as leptokurtosis (peakedness) and heteroscedasticity (non-constant variance).

The basic steps of a Monte Carlo framework include a) fit a model to the existing data; b) calculate the model residuals; c) create a new realization of the existing data by adding a random draw of residuals back to the original model predictions; d) fit a new model to this new realization to estimate or predict; and e) repeat *n* times. This approach provides *n* estimates for each new data point and the distribution created by the *n* estimates can be used to quantify uncertainty. This distribution of estimates can be used as input into another model or otherwise combined with other observations to link uncertainty from multiple sources. Estimates from this approach can be combined efficiently to allow for spatial aggregation of uncertainty estimates, which often require dubious assumptions when done analytically. The downside to this approach is that it is data and computationally intensive.

Conclusion

Inventory planning is an optimization problem. Sampling error can be minimized for a given cost or the cost can be minimized for a desired level of maximum acceptable error. Monitoring costs need to be smaller than potential financial benefits. It is critical, however, to identify and manage all sources of error from early in the project. The IPCC should consider revisiting the 95% confidence interval due the potentially high cost of a monitoring system to meet this requirement.

Several issues must be addressed during implementation of an uncertainty accounting. Complete accounting of uncertainty is important, but agreement is needed as to what the project boundaries are (i.e. which sources of uncertainty should be included). Collaborative effort is required for complete uncertainty accounting. Sharing models and data is required among project members.

Uncertainty Issues in Forest Monitoring: All You Wanted to Know About Uncertainties and Never Dared to Ask

Michael Köhl[1], Charles Scott[2], and Daniel Plugge[3]

Abstract

Uncertainties are a composite of errors arising from observations and the appropriateness of models. An error budget approach can be used to identify and accumulate the sources of errors to estimate change in emissions between two points in time. Various forest monitoring approaches can be used to estimate the changes in emissions due to deforestation and forest degradation. Sample-based approaches often combine remotely sensed data with probabilistic field samples to develop design-based estimates. The survey designer must choose between a host of imagery sources, sampling designs, plot designs, allometric models of tree biomass, and estimators. Each choice has implications for uncertainty and cost. We describe three general areas for improvement: 1) inventory planning, sampling design optimization, 2) technological development focused on use of imagery, and 3) tree biomass estimation.

[1]Institute of World Forestry, University of Hamburg, Leuschnerstr.91, 21031 Hamburg, Germany
[2]National Inventory & Monitoring Applications Center, USDA Forest Service, 11 Campus Blvd., Suite 200 Newton Square, PA 19073
[3]Institute of World Forestry, von Thünen-Institute, Leuschnerst.91, 21031 Hamburg, Germany
Corresponding author: ctscott@fs.fed.us

Application of a Monte Carlo Framework with Bootstrapping for Quantification of Uncertainty in Baseline Map of Carbon Emissions from Deforestation in Tropical Regions

*William Salas[1] and Steve Hagen[1]

Abstract

This presentation will provide an overview of an approach for quantifying uncertainty in spatial estimates of carbon emission from land use change. We generate uncertainty bounds around our final emissions estimate using a randomized, Monte Carlo (MC)-style sampling technique. This approach allows us to combine uncertainty from different sources without making assumptions about the distribution of the underlying data. We incorporate uncertainty from the following components: Estimates of forest loss; Estimates of aboveground biomass; and Estimates of belowground biomass. In each scenario of the MC simulation, forested pixels (1-km) within each 18.5-km block (the scale of MODIS-derived deforestation data) are selected randomly until the total cleared area estimated within the block is reached. Carbon stock information for the cleared pixels is then used to calculate an emissions estimate associated with forest loss for that scenario. Iterating through scenarios for each block results in a distribution of emissions associated with the estimated level of forest loss. This distribution is then used to define uncertainty based on a set confidence level.

*Based on Harris et al., Baseline Map of Carbon Emissions from Deforestation in Tropical Regions. Science, 2012; 336 (6088): 1573 DOI: 10.1126/science.1217962
[1]Applied Geosolutions, 87 Packers Falls Rd., Durham, NH 03924
Corresponding author: wsalas@appliedgeosolutions.com

Integration of Monitoring Techniques

Water buffalo skid trail in degraded forest, Con Cuong District, Nghe An Province, Viet Nam.
(Photo: Leif Mortenson)

Section Summary

Yoshiyuki Kiyono[1] and Rick Turner[2]

Techniques for monitoring deforestation and associated changes to forest carbon stocks are widespread and well published. In contrast, techniques for monitoring forest degradation are relatively untested in developing countries despite their inclusion in UNFCCC REDD+ negotiations. In the Mekong countries, forest degradation may contribute a substantial portion of the total carbon losses from forests. There is a critical need to assess approaches for monitoring forest degradation, particularly at the sub-national level. One potential obstacle in assessing monitoring approaches for the region is the lack of consensus on the definition of forest degradation. In addition to a common definition, management objectives must be determined, i.e. what desired threshold of degradation needs to be detected. Monitoring approaches should recognize common themes among countries regarding drivers of degradation, while taking into account the unique circumstances of each country, especially in regard to capacity for operationalizing any recommended protocols.

Monitoring Carbon Stock in Areas Subject to Shifting Agriculture

Conversion of natural forest to agricultural land is one of the most influential land use changes on the loss of both carbon stock and biodiversity in ecosystems. However, forestland designated for agricultural use can sometimes continue to be classified as forest when the residual amount of tree canopy cover remaining meets the accepted definition of forested land. Vegetation change induced by shortening of the fallow period of the slash-and-burn (swidden) agricultural cycle may result in increased forest degradation or eventually deforestation if the fallow period is too short to allow vegetation to grow back enough to meet the definition of forest land. Forests in northern Lao PDR are subject to intensive slash-and-burn agriculture and have been degraded by shortening of the fallow period. For such forest degradation, a practical approach to monitor carbon stock change is to use the parameter of plant community age. Destructive sampling for allometric equations for bamboo was conducted and a model using plant community age to monitor forest degradation was developed in Lao PDR (Kiyono et al. 2007). For cyclic land use that includes a tree-removal stage, chronosequential changes in carbon stock can be estimated by determining the ages and spatial distribution of cleared land. Long-term ecosystem carbon stock change under different land use patterns can be simulated (Inoue et al. 2010). To estimate carbon stock under a shifting agriculture chronosequence, an integration of both ground-based measurement and remote sensing data are needed.

---

[1]Forestry and Forest Products Research Institute (FFPRI), Matsunosato 1, Tsukuba, Ibaraki 305-8687, Japan
[2]US Forest Service, Tongass National Forest, 8510 Mendenhall Loop Road, Juneau AK, 99801
Corresponding author: kiono@ffpri.affrc.go.jp

Forest carbon stock can be calculated by multiplying forest area with averaged carbon stocks per land area for given land use. Kiyono et al. (2011) assessed non-destructive approaches for monitoring anthropogenic greenhouse gas (GHG) emissions from tropical dry-land forest under the influence of various forms of human intervention. A matrix was developed to rank the suitability of each approach, including costs, potential to obtaining data in a large land area, technical difficulties, and applicability to various anthropogenic activities, including degradation drivers such as reducing fallow period of slash-and-burn agriculture, logging, and fuel wood collection. This matrix is complex and comprehensive; however, the assessments of the various approaches need to be examined in greater detail. According to the matrix rankings, no reasonable remote-sensing methods exist at present to monitor carbon loss due to forest degradation in forests with high biomass. To enable practical and frequent monitoring of all types of forests, it is vital to devise a new methodology to detect changes in high-biomass forests.

Monitoring Forest Degradation at the Sub-National Level

The Lowering Emissions in Asia's Forests (LEAF) program of the United States Agency for International Development/Regional Development Mission for Asia (USAID/RDMA) recently asked the United States Forest Service to assess options for monitoring forest degradation at sub-national levels in three Mekong countries: Cambodia, Lao PDR, and Vietnam. The three focus areas were the Central Cardamom Protection Forest in southwestern Cambodia, the Xamtai and Viengxay Districts in the Houaphanh province of northern Lao PDR, and the district of Con Cuong, in Nghe An Province of north-central Vietnam. The study areas included all forested lands regardless of ownership or land use designation. The assessments followed a similar conceptual framework, which includes: 1) define biomass references for monitoring in each forest strata of interest, 2) identify and assess the scale and intensity of forest degradation drivers, and 3) identify and assess monitoring approaches based on defined biomass change thresholds. Three main monitoring approaches, including ground-based field measurements, remotely sensed imagery, and predictive modeling, were assessed using a qualitative ranking system. The results were then used to develop an integrated monitoring system for each study area that combined applicable elements of all three approaches. Emphasis was placed on cost efficiency by using existing infrastructure and data sources as much as possible. For each recommended monitoring system, workflow diagrams were developed which illustrate the relationships between the various data sources and analysis methods.

One issue that emerged during the forest degradation monitoring workshop discussion was: should a monitoring system be designed to efficiently utilize existing capacity only, or should capacity building be a part of the recommendations? The monitoring systems for all three study areas include reasonably attainable recommendations for building capacity necessary for implementing monitoring. However, capacity-building goals may need to be set higher, if increased capacity is needed in order to implement a robust monitoring system. As REDD+ programs are implemented, increased funding may become available to support forest degradation monitoring. Therefore, flexibility should be incorporated into recommended monitoring systems to provide the ability to adjust to changing institutional capacities. Monitoring systems should also be implemented in an iterative fashion with full consultation of relevant stakeholders, with the initial recommendations used as a starting point from which refined protocols and methods are developed according to local circumstances and conditions.

Practicalities of Methodologies in Monitoring Forest Degradation in the Tropics

Yoshiyuki Kiyono[1]

Abstract

Conversion of natural forest to agricultural land is one of the most important forms of land-use change affecting both carbon stock and biodiversity. When the agricultural land contains trees, e.g. fallow-land forest of slash-and-burn agriculture, the conversion can be categorized into forest degradation when the forest definition covers such vegetation. One practical method to monitor carbon stock change is an approach using a parameter for plant community age. For cyclic land use that includes clear-cutting stage, from which chronosequential changes in carbon stock can be estimated by determining time and spatial-distribution of cleared land. Inoue et al. (2007) detected slash-and-burn fields using a time-series of Landsat images and a model containing the parameter for plant community age, and estimated chronosequential changes in carbon stock in fallow land in northern Laos. Kiyono et al. (2011) examined non-destructive methodologies for practicalities in monitoring anthropogenic greenhouse gas (GHG) emissions from tropical dry-land forest under the influence of various forms of human intervention. No reasonable remote sensing methods exist for monitoring at a large scale the amount of carbon loss by forest conversion and logging in forests with high-biomass. To enable practical and frequent monitoring of all types of forests impacted by humans, it is vital to devise a new methodology to detect changes in high-biomass forests.

[1]Forestry and Forest Products Research Institute (FFPRI), Matsunosato 1, Tsukuba, Ibaraki 305-8687, Japan
Corresponding author: kiono@ffpri.affrc.go.jp

Forest Degradation Sub-National Assessments: Monitoring Options for Cambodia, Lao PDR, and Vietnam

Rick Turner[1], James Halperin[2], Patricia Manley[3], and Leif Mortenson[4]

Abstract

Techniques for monitoring deforestation and associated changes to forest carbon stocks are widespread and well published. In contrast, techniques for monitoring forest degradation are relatively untested in developing countries despite their inclusion in UNFCCC REDD+ negotiations. The Lowering Emissions in Asia's Forests (LEAF) program of the United States Agency for International Development/Regional Development Mission for Asia (USAID/RDMA) is working to address issues and challenges regarding forest degradation monitoring. The United States Forest Service was asked by LEAF and its partner organizations to assess options for monitoring forest degradation at sub-national levels in three Mekong countries: Cambodia, Lao PDR, and Vietnam. The study areas included the Central Cardamom Protection Forest in southwestern Cambodia (401,000 Ha), the Xamtai and Viengxay Districts in the Houaphanh province of northern Lao PDR (541,000 Ha), and the district of Con Cuong, in Nghe An Province of north-central Vietnam (175,000 Ha).

To assess monitoring options in the study areas, a conceptual framework was developed that includes three basic steps: 1) define biomass references for monitoring in each forest strata of interest, 2) identify and assess the scale and intensity of forest degradation drivers, and 3) identify and assess monitoring approaches based on defined biomass change thresholds. We evaluated three main approaches, including ground-based field measurements, remotely sensed imagery, and predictive modeling. Potential variants of each approach were assessed for each study area using a qualitative ranking system. The results were then used to develop an integrated monitoring system for each study area combining elements of all three approaches. Each monitoring system includes specific recommendations for integrating the three monitoring approaches that will likely meet the stated objectives. Each monitoring system must consider the important drivers of degradation in the study area, the operational circumstances for monitoring, and the expected capacity for implementation. A critical next step is implementing and testing the monitoring systems in the three study areas as proof-of-concept for potential application to other geographic areas in the region.

---

[1]US Forest Service, Tongass National Forest, 8510 Mendenhall Loop Road, Juneau AK, 99801
[2]Center for International Forestry Research, Lusaka, Zambia
[3]US Forest Service, Pacific Southwest Research Station, 2480 Carson Road, Placerville, CA 95667
[4]US Forest Service, Pacific Northwest Research Station, 620 SW Main St. Suite 400, Portland, OR 97205
Corresponding author: rlturner@fs.fed.us

Detection of Forest Degradation Drivers

Field evaluation, Con Cuong District, Nghe An Province, Viet Nam
(Photo: Leif Mortenson)

Summary of Small Group Discussions

Patricia Manley[1]

Workshop participants were asked to address sets of questions in small group discussions, which were subsequently brought to the entire group for discussion. The first set of questions was directed at identifying a set of degradation activities that could be a primary focus for developing or refining methods and techniques for monitoring:

- What drivers and degradation sources can be detected?
- What methods are most effective at detection?
- What are the challenges and opportunities in detecting degradation?

Drivers

The definition and classification of drivers and degradation activities continues to present challenges. Currently there are no international agreements through IPCC or the UNFCCC on how to classify forest degradation drivers. However, relevant to a REDD+ mechanism, there are several ways to classify the activities that contribute to degradation of forests. Workshop participants differed in their opinions as to whether drivers were the correct focus, or whether the focus should simply be on human extraction of forest products that reduces forest carbon stocks. Despite these differences, all agreed that activities needed to be identified for monitoring degradation.

Traditional forest monitoring methods (remote sensing, ground-based field measurements) are most often used to assess changes in forest structure and quality. Understanding which direct drivers are present is the most important first step towards identifying possible monitoring methods. Participants of the workshop identified four primary and four secondary categories of drivers that are prevalent and substantial contributors to carbon loss in the forests of Southeast Asia:

- Primary
    - Selective logging: commercial planned, commercial unplanned, and domestic (customary)
    - Fuelwood gathering: commercial and domestic (customary)
    - Shifting cultivation
    - Conversion to plantations (if using a definition of forest where plantation is not considered forest)
- Secondary
    - Human induced forest fire
    - Non-timber forest products (e.g., yellow vine)
    - Access
    - Grazing

---

[1]US Forest Service, Pacific Southwest Research Station, 2480 Carson Road, Placerville, CA 95667
Corresponding author: pmanley@fs.fed.us

There were a few differences in how the groups defined selective logging, with some separating single tree removal from multiple tree harvest, but generally single tree removal was synonymous with domestic or customary use. Individual trees are removed for a variety of applications, including personal use as housing material and for sale. The activities considered secondary were primarily a function of their prevalence, as opposed to the impact of individual occurrence on carbon. In landscapes in which these activities are prevalent, they could be considered primary.

Field Methods

The participants identified the primary field-based data sources that could detect and describe the primary degradation activities as the following:
- Forest management unit inventories
- Permanent sampling plots
- Change detection inventory
- Interviews/secondary data
- Participatory monitoring
- Temporary sampling plots

Although a diversity of opinions were expressed, the two groups that addressed field methods agreed that permanent plots and temporary plots both had important contributions to meeting monitoring information needs. Permanent plots provided measures of growth and accurate change detection for vigor, disease, and harvest. Cost was identified as the primary limiting factor for permanent plots – both the cost to install and the cost to relocate and remeasure in a precise manner. Temporary sampling plots have strengths and limitations that are complementary to permanent plots – faster to install for a given budget, additional plots can be measured, but they lack data on growth and have additional sources of error in estimates of change. Participatory monitoring was considered by most, but not all participants as a secondary source of data as opposed to a primary given the uncertainty associated with how to maintain and validate data quality.

Remote-Sensing Methods

Group participants identified a wide range of applications for remote sensing data in meeting forest carbon monitoring needs, with the primary focus being on selective logging. One of the contributions remote sensing can make to monitoring of selective logging was indirectly, through the detection of roads, skid trails, and landing areas. Degradation risk and predicted intensity of selective logging in association with these readily detected features is a unique contribution that remote sensing can make. Direct detections of selective logging, including individual tree removal, are more challenging, but can be estimated based on detected changes in canopy cover using combinations of high and moderate resolution imagery. At least one of the groups felt that remote sensing could offer reliable change detection, early warning information on shifts in use, detailed information on threatened areas, and frequent repeatability in areas that warranted it for whatever reason. Direct detections for plantations are accomplishable with low resolution imagery, and are possible with more advanced methodology for shifting cultivation and fire, but discussions were primarily limited to selective logging.

Ideally, remote sensing would be the primary source, if not a sole source, of data for monitoring forest degradation. It is objective, spatially consistent and comprehensive, repeatable with minimal error, and does not require capacity building across as large a population of technicians as is needed for ground based monitoring. In general terms, remote sensing faces many challenges in detecting degradation, including clouds, topography, access, cost, and capacity. Opportunities for overcoming these challenges lie in technological advances that offer higher resolution imagery at reduced costs to users and overall more accessible technology – a process that takes place over an uncertain time scale and over which most practitioners do not have control. In the meantime, practical challenges posed by existing technology need to be addressed.

Technical challenges associated with detecting selective logging fell into three categories: 1) visual interpretation; 2) object-based image classification; and 3) spectral un-mixing. Visual interpretation challenges included short-duration of detectability of canopy gaps in many cases, ability to obtain sufficient cloud-free images over a short period of time, steep topography, consistency among observers over time, voluminous data associated with higher resolution imagery, and scaling up. Object-based image classification can also be challenging, namely effectively setting up routines for segmentation. Spectral un-mixing challenges included obtaining ancillary data to correctly classify local land cover classes, consistency in technology and interpretation, and consistently interpreting conditions in steep terrain (i.e., topographic illumination allometry).

Finally, feasibility challenges were identified, primarily in association with high resolution imagery. They included availability, access (for LiDAR), frequency needed to detect ephemeral canopy gaps, narrow window of time for data collection in deciduous forests, cost to obtain imagery, cost to process imagery, local capacity to process and interpret data (people, knowledge and hardware), ability to scale data to provide useful interpretations at multiple scales (e.g., "scaling-up"), and the difficulty in linking observed changes to specific drivers.

Conclusions

Challenges in detecting degradation with remote-sensing were numerous, and generally indicated that remotes sensing plays a central role in detecting and monitoring primary sources of degradation; however it must be used in conjunction with field-based data sources, statistical modeling, and decision support tools in order to achieve an adequate level of detectability and a reliable characterization of forest carbon to address emissions. Similarly, field-based sampling, although technically simple, is labor and time intensive, making it inefficient as a singular approach to monitoring degradation.

Challenges in designing and implementing field sampling for monitoring carbon paralleled the strengths and weaknesses of the methods – the intersection of time, cost, and the data yielded and its value. The lack of a clear singular best approach seems to indicate that a multi-pronged approach will be most effective, one that is tailored to meet the needs of a given landscape, and one that can be adapted over time to be more efficient and effective as opportunities arise. The overarching challenge then becomes to determine at what spatial scales monitoring approaches need to be similar, and in what ways do they need to be consistent over time. For example, an optimal monitoring approach for a district in one part of a country may look very different than an optimal monitoring approach for a district in another part of the country as a function of capacity, terrain, land use, etc. However, in order to maximize the utility of the monitoring data to address a range of questions about forest conditions, biodiversity, ecosystem services, and drivers (i.e., to maximize co-benefits), as much consistency as possible is desirable at province, multi-province, ecoregional and national scales. Finding a balance in these objectives will be enhanced by a few key demonstration projects that highlight how to assess and select optimal monitoring designs. A two-pronged, phased approach to implementation (design, capacity building, data acquisition, and analysis/interpretation) that simultaneously targets the development of efficient and effective monitoring at local scales (e.g., districts or provinces) and the development of an effective national inventory will enhance the probability that solid, forward progress is made toward meeting the information needs of REDD+ and realizing multiple co-benefits.

Monitoring Objectives and Thresholds

Pu Mat National Park, Con Cuong District, Nghe An
Province, Viet Nam
(Photo: Leif Mortenson)

Summary of Small Group Discussions

Patricia Manley[1]

Workshop participants were asked to address sets of questions in small group discussions, which were subsequently brought to the entire group for discussion. The second set of questions was directed at identifying a set of degradation activities that could be a primary focus for developing or refining methods and techniques for monitoring:

- What are realistic monitoring objectives and what are the thresholds needed to assess change?

- What are the appropriate scales to target for monitoring?

- What challenges and opportunities exist for accomplishing these objectives?

The objectives were defined in terms of measures of condition, and thresholds were defined as minimum magnitudes of change that monitoring should attempt to detect with reasonable statistical power and precision. General tenets for identifying realistic goals were developed by the groups. They were outlined for each of three topics.

Capacity Building

- Work from where we are today, which varies by country

- Build on existing institutions and expertise

- Build on existing reporting structures

- Need to build capacity at all scales – need to identify what capacity is needed at what scale

- Target building computing capacity (GIS, remote sensing) at national and provincial scale

- A phased approach is prudent for capacity building

Setting Thresholds

- Degradation, afforestation, deforestation rates are relevant contexts for thresholds

- Assess relative change from existing baseline conditions

- Target thresholds should be informed by costs versus benefits

[1]US Forest Service, Pacific Southwest Research Station, 2480 Carson Road, Placerville, CA 95667.
Corresponding author: pmanley@fs.fed.us

- Test and refine target thresholds over time (e.g., through data analysis and modeling)

- Reporting frequency should be clearly identified – no more than 5 year intervals

- Shifting cultivation can have significant temporary effects on some measure that could mask smaller more permanent effects

Implementation

- A phased approach is prudent for implementation

- Use a "no regrets" approach to guide investments in implementation, meaning they will be useful no matter what else gets accomplished

Specific objectives and thresholds identified by the discussion groups varied by the type of degradation activity. Targeted activities were those most readily monitored through readily available remote sensing or field data collection methods, and included: selective logging, fuel wood, and swiddening. Fire was identified as another activity for which thresholds could be identified, but the group did not have the opportunity to address fire in any detail.

Selective logging was defined here as activities that resulted in wood products (e.g., lumber, poles for houses). Planned commercial logging typically targets larger trees with diameters > 50 cm. Thresholds for this activity minimally would detect reductions of trees >50 cm in diameter and reductions of >50% of the biomass per hectare. Frequency of resample was identified as a maximum of 30 years, assuming that reentry for commercial logging would not be more frequent than that. However, frequency of resample most likely would be a function of reentry rates and required reporting frequencies specific to the area.

Unplanned logging represents forest uses for domestic or commercial uses. Unplanned logging can occur in areas that are also subject to planned commercial logging. Tree removal for customary uses typically targets smaller trees with < 50 cm diameters, limited primarily by equipment (e.g., machete, buffalo). Target thresholds for areas subject to unplanned selective logging would be loss of trees >30 cm in diameter and reductions of >30% of the biomass per hectare. Frequency of resample could be any feasible time period, given that tree removal in most areas is occurring throughout the year and every year. Of course, over time accessibility and need will vary, so some areas that were not subject to unplanned logging could begin to be logged. Given the dynamic nature of tree extraction activities, we recommend a minimum 5-year resample or a resample frequency coincident with other forest monitoring measurements for reporting purposes (whichever is shorter) to provide a comprehensive snapshot of conditions across contiguous landscape.

Fuel wood removal commonly would occur in the same areas as unplanned logging, given that both are a function of access and need, and the same conditions are favorable to both activities. Therefore, we recommend that the thresholds set for unplanned logging be applied to any forested area with a reasonable risk of degradation by unplanned activities. Degradation risk can be determined by assessing the factors that directly and indirectly drive unplanned logging and intensive fuel wood collection, such as access, local population size, local poverty levels, etc. (see Chapter 1).

Swiddening (i.e., slash and burn shifting agriculture) involves a temporary deforested condition over variable sized areas for a variable number of years. Once the agricultural activity is stopped, the assumption is that the area will recover at the same pace as one would expect after a natural disturbance. The ability to detect swiddening will depend on the size of the clearing, the duration of use, and the density of areas cleared for swiddening at any point in time. Generally, medium resolution Landsat data can detect >1-hectare areas that are maintained for at least 3 years (providing a 4-5 year window of detection). The use of chronosequencing models can help to estimate change in biomass over short periods of time, when combined with accurate land use/land cover change maps. High resolution remote sensing data can enhance these estimates by detecting smaller clearings and refining models. Landscape attributes and village locations can be used to identify areas of high risk of degradation from swiddening, which in turn may influence the frequency and intensity of repeated measures.

The challenges and opportunities for identifying monitoring objectives, and thresholds in particular, are many. The primary challenge and the most limiting factor is capacity. The group noted that starting with existing conditions, both ecologically and institutionally, is fundamental to making progress. In most countries, this means starting at basic levels of acquisition of equipment, data, and training. Investments in national and provincial monitoring data and data management/interpretation abilities are essential. The limitation of national and provincial-level investments is that they do not build capacity at the ground level, and as a result the benefits are mostly at those larger scales. Demonstration projects provide a complementary investment to larger-scale investments in that they take place in and involve local communities and staff. Local involvement is one important criterion to successfully determining forest conditions at a level of resolution and reliability that can be used for REDD+ monitoring, and that can help identify problems in a timely manner such that policies and other tools can be put in place to achieve the desired objectives of maintaining or increasing forest cover and forest quality.

Regional Themes and Next Steps

Con Cuong District, Nghe An Province, Viet Nam.
(Photo: Leif Mortenson)

Small Group Discussions and Conclusions

Rick Turner[1]

At the conclusion of the workshop, a breakout group session discussed common themes that had emerged regarding forest degradation monitoring in the Southeast Asia region. The participants were also asked to list any important issues that may not have been sufficiently addressed during the workshop and that may require further discussion, and recommendations for next steps in moving forest degradation monitoring forward in the region were developed.

Regional Themes

One common theme that emerged during the workshop was that monitoring methods based on only one approach (e.g. remote sensing, ground-based measurements, predictive modeling) would likely be insufficient to provide robust estimates of biomass change due to degradation activities. Rather, an integrated monitoring system, combining elements of two or more approaches, would likely be more flexible in adapting to local and national circumstances and capacities. While regional consistency in monitoring methods is desirable, a single monitoring system approach may not fit all circumstances. The main drivers of forest degradation, as well as existing institutional capacities for implementing monitoring programs, can vary greatly among countries in the region. In addition, countries may apply different definitions for forest degradation, as well as different thresholds for detection. How degradation is defined will influence selection of methods and data sources for a particular monitoring system. Demonstration projects should be implemented in multiple countries and forest types to provide a comparison and proof-of-concept of various approaches.

Several needs were identified for implementing degradation monitoring in the region. Although a few REDD+ projects have been established in limited areas, there is a need to scale up to larger landscapes that are more relevant to estimating overall emissions and that would provide more efficient management, monitoring, and reporting. It is essential that current REDD+ projects include degradation monitoring in their monitoring programs to avoid omitting a potentially large source of emissions from their estimates. It was also recognized that institutional capacity for monitoring needs to be strengthened in all countries in the region in order to support a robust, long-term monitoring program. Some identified technical needs included the development of botanical skills of field measurement crews, more consistent forest vegetation classifications and accurate forest type maps, and the development of more reliable allometric biomass equations for common forest types.

---

[1]US Forest Service, Tongass National Forest, 8510 Mendenhall Loop Road, Juneau AK, 99801.
Corresponding author: rlturner@fs.fed.us

Issues for Further Discussion

Some important issues needing further collaboration include the need for a more precise definition of forest degradation. Without a well-defined concept of degradation, establishing meaningful monitoring objectives and thresholds will be problematic. There is a need to determine criteria to identify conditions under which swiddening and tree plantations may degrade the ability of forests to store carbon. Additionally, consensus on the definition of forest is needed to properly address the effects of swiddening and tree plantations on carbon monitoring. The significance of fire should also be more thoroughly assessed, including possible interactions with other degradation drivers such as selective logging and shifting agriculture. In addition to biomass loss, the gain from forest regrowth over time after disturbance must be assessed to more accurately estimate net carbon stock change in Greenhouse Gas reporting. Just as with deforestation, leakage may become an issue in forest degradation, as management to reduce degradation activities in one area can potentially shift those activities to other landscapes within a country, or across national boundaries.

Much of the discussion on degradation monitoring methods focused on remote sensing and ground-based field measurements. Although predictive modeling was addressed as a third monitoring approach, more information is needed to understand how modeling can be combined with the other methods to develop a more robust monitoring system, especially in areas where obtaining remote sensing or ground-based data is difficult due to technical or capacity constraints. Much valuable information could be obtained from case studies in which predictive modeling is an integral part of the monitoring system. Quantitative comparisons of cost versus accuracy and precision among the various monitoring approaches would also be informative.

The participants felt that more discussion should be devoted to developing the institutional framework and governance needed to support a degradation monitoring program. Although it is important to build technical capacity within countries to implement monitoring, efforts also need to be made to ensure that technical information is relayed to policy makers to facilitate better understanding and encourage institutional commitment of resources to monitoring.

Next Steps

A recommended next step in initiating forest degradation monitoring in the region is to implement demonstration projects that aim to estimate and monitor forest degradation as case studies, most appropriately at the sub-national level. These projects should integrate various monitoring approaches into a system that is responsive to local degradation drivers and appropriate to the local and national circumstances. Logical sites for initial implementation of degradation monitoring projects could be the sub-national focus areas assessed by LEAF in Cambodia (Central Cardamon Protection Forest), Laos (Houaphanh Province), and Vietnam (Nghe An Province). Implementing the three demonstration projects would help to refine model parameters and workflows, as well as provide data on the contribution of degradation to the total emissions profile. It may also be instructive to identify similar on-going projects in other regions as additional sources of information.

Another important next step is increasing efforts to build technical and financial capacity for monitoring in the region. It is important to determine the minimum requirements for monitoring forest degradation. Potential donor countries and organizations will need to be involved in determining minimum requirements, as the purpose of monitoring is to ensure that credits issued for carbon stored in forests is verifiable. Recipient countries and organizations are in need of cost assessments for implementing and maintaining a monitoring program, including costs of various monitoring approaches relative to benefits, i.e. carbon credits.

Facilitating technical transfer is important to ensure that the most current research is incorporated into monitoring systems and the consistency is maintained across the region as much as practicable. One recommended approach is developing regional instructional manuals, including ground-based field measurement, remote sensing imagery analysis, and predictive modeling methods. Another potential conduit for technology transfer could be technical assistance initiatives such as SilvaCarbon, a global USAID-funded program aimed to build knowledge and capacity in forest carbon monitoring. This workshop can also form the foundation for continued dialogue, networking, and data sharing. Future workshops could be planned to share lessons learned from implementation of monitoring projects.

Conclusions

James Halperin[1] and David Ganz[2]

Monitoring forest degradation is a complex process that needs to account for a wide variety of forest characteristics, human activities, and programmatic resources in order to achieve reliable results. This workshop sought to deepen understanding of monitoring forest degradation as it relates to these issues by: a) discussing implications from definitions related to operationalizing forest monitoring degradation; b) assessing case studies with current, and emerging, best practices to detect and monitor forest degradation; and, c) identifying ways forward for forest degradation monitoring demonstration activities.

Forest degradation definitions do matter. However, not all experts agree to what degree definitions need to be clearly established before implementing monitoring activities. For example, a monitoring program generally sets thresholds for detectability and statistical precision when it may be unknown if these attributes are achievable. The process of monitoring often reveals data and trends that were not previously known and refinement of definitions can occur through implementation. Consensus from the workshop does indicate that forest biomass and biomass change must be the key parameters of interest in monitoring forest degradation for REDD+ initiatives.

Case studies that focus on forest degradation monitoring are limited, especially those which focus on Southeast Asia. Efforts to assess and estimate forest degradation must be responsive to the direct drivers that impact forest biomass. The main direct drivers of degradation are selective logging for timber, harvesting for fuel wood, and shifting cultivation. Selective logging has received the majority of attention, as evidenced in the case studies presented. Methods formulated to monitor forest biomass after selective logging range from remote sensing, ground based field measurements, to development of Emission Factors that standardize the impacts of biomass per unit area.

Effective methods to detect forest degradation at adequate levels of precision and repeatability, and at scales of interest, remain elusive. Remote sensing methodologies are often hampered by persistent cloud cover, quick canopy cover re-growth, a lack of expertise in automated processing and/or a lack access to imagery with spatial resolution at scales relevant to degradation drivers. However, remotely sensed imagery is consistently available and covers wide areas that often cannot be accessed. Coupled with ground based field measurements to provide biomass estimates, the use and applicability of remotely sensed data to monitor forest degradation cannot be understated.

While this workshop provided ample lessons from case studies that can help promote forest degradation monitoring initiatives, six gaps in current knowledge remain. First, modeling approaches that integrate both remotely sensed data and ground based field

---

[1]Center for International Forestry Research, Lusaka, Zambia
[2]LEAF Asia, Liberty Square, Suite 2002, 287 Silom Road, Bangrak, Bangkok, 10500 Thailand
Corresponding author: j.halperin@cgiar.org

measurement data rarely have been tested in tropical forests, if at all (albeit commonly used in temperate forests). Second, fire as a driver of forest degradation is poorly understood. Tropical fire ecology is an undeveloped field of science and little is known of biomass dynamics as it relates to fire regimes. Third, planned selective harvesting for timber impacts forest biomass dynamics in unpredictable ways. Likewise, it is debatable if this type of harvesting can be considered degradation when compared to unplanned harvesting. Fourth, tree plantations may be considered forests in some countries, and agricultural crops in others. In this context, it is possible that conversion could be considered either degradation or deforestation. This raises an important question pertaining to biodiversity safeguards. Fifth, forest re-growth after disturbance needs attention in order to account for net changes in forest biomass dynamics. Lastly, forest degradation monitoring may be feasible and practical at some scales in some places while not others. However, monitoring results will ultimately need to nest within national frameworks of emissions reporting. There is a large gap in knowledge of nesting approaches to indicate how monitoring at sub-national scale can inform national monitoring and reporting initiatives, and vice-versa.

Several key messages emerged from this workshop with strong consensus. The first key message is that demonstration activities to develop forest degradation monitoring methods and tools need more widespread implementation. Demonstration activities should strive to simultaneously address two or more of the knowledge gaps as mentioned above. These activities should occur at scales relevant to national reporting requirements but also where sufficient resources can be directed to provide adequate lessons learned. Further, demonstration activities need to address a range of drivers, forest types and conditions, and socio-economic circumstances in order to compare approaches, input data sources, and costs- all in relation to acceptable levels of precision. Successful demonstrations of forest degradation monitoring are not easy to achieve. Yet they are necessary for providing clarity into future operationalization of forest degradation monitoring programs.

Secondly, forest degradation monitoring programs must be sensitive to the degradation drivers that impact forest biomass. For example, selective logging for timber in tropical wet forest generally has a large impact on biomass in relatively small areas. Harvesting trees for fuel wood has a smaller impact on biomass across large areas. In this context, there may be no 'one size fits all' approach to methodology development. Remote sensing and ground based field measurement approaches for selective logging may not be appropriate for fuel wood harvesting, and vice versa.

Thirdly, capacity building and strengthening within partner institutions and civil society organizations needs to incorporate long-term solutions that aim high. Coupling researchers with practitioners and land use managers provides an effective framework for integrating advanced methodologies into forest monitoring programs. Lessons learned are most likely to be meaningful when accomplished through experience combined with trial and error. Programs addressing the key questions of forest degradation monitoring will ultimately reduce costs of technology and methodology transfer, through institutionalizing advanced monitoring frameworks.

Forest degradation monitoring requires a depth of knowledge and understanding in many different disciplines including remote sensing, forest biometrics and mensuration, sampling theory and strategy, ecology, and modeling. The interdisciplinary nature of forest degradation monitoring makes it a challenging professional endeavor and requires significant commitments in terms of time and resources. This workshop aimed high in bringing together experts for achieving consensus on forest monitoring definitions, thresholds, and methodologies. The achievements included a common definition of the main parameter of interest; consensus that integration of data sources is crucial to take advantage of multiple inputs, and that monitoring approaches must be demonstrated and compared at multiple sites through project initiatives before being operationalized. The workshop organizers hope that the insights and ideas brought forward by this diverse group of experts will be able to influence forest degradation monitoring design initiatives well into the future.

Literature Cited

FAO (Food and Agricultural Organization). 2005. State of the World's Forests (Rome: UNFAO).

FAO (Food and Agricultural Organization). 2010. Global Forest Resources Assesment 2010 Country Report Indonesia *Forest Resources Assessment (FRA)* (Rome: UNFAO)

Inoue, Y., J. Qi, A. Olioso, Y. Kiyono, T. Horie, H. Asai, K. Saito, Y. Ochiai, T. Shiraiwa, and L. Douangsavanh. 2007. Traceability of slash- and- burn land- use history using optical satellite sensor imagery: a basis for chronosequential assessment of ecosystem carbon stock in Laos." *International Journal of Remote Sensing* 28(24): 5641-5647.

Inoue, Y., Y. Kiyono, H. Asai, Y. Ochiai, J. Qi, A. Olioso, T. Shiraiwa, T. Horie, K. Saito, L. Dounagsavanh. 2010. Assessing land-use and carbon stock in slash-and-burn ecosystems in tropical mountains of Laos based on time-series satellite images. International Journal of Applied Earth Observation and Geoinformation 12: 287-297.

Kissinger, G., Herold, M., & De Sy, V. 2012. Drivers of deforestation and forest degradation: a synthesis report for REDD+ policymakers. Lexeme Consulting, Vancouver, Canada.

Kiyono, Y., Y. Ochiai, Y. Chiba, H. Asai, K. Saito, T. Shiraiwa, T. Horie, V. Songnoukhai, V. Navongxai, Y. Inoue. 2007. Predicting chronosequential changes in carbon stocks of pachymorph bamboo communities in slash-and-burn agricultural fallow, northern Lao People's Democratic Republic. Journal of Forest Research 12:371-383.

Kiyono Y., S. Saito, T. Takahashi, J. Toriyama, Y. Awaya, H. Asai, N. Furuya, Y. Ochiai, Y. Inoue, T. Sato, C. Sophal, P. Sam, B. Tith, E. Ito, A.C. Siregar, M. Matsumoto. 2011. Practicalities of non-destructive methodologies in monitoring anthropogenic greenhouse gas emissions from tropical forests under the influence of human intervention. JARQ 45(2): 233-242.

This publication is available online at www.fs.fed.us/psw/. You may also order additional copies of it by sending your mailing information in label form through one of the following means. Please specify the publication title and series number.

Fort Collins Service Center

Web site	http://www.fs.fed.us/psw/
Telephone	(970) 498-1392
FAX	(970) 498-1122
E-mail	rschneider@fs.fed.us
Mailing address	Publications Distribution
	Rocky Mountain Research Station
	240 West Prospect Road
	Fort Collins, CO 80526-2098

Pacific Southwest Research Station
800 Buchanan Street
Albany, CA 94710

Federal Recycling Program
Printed on Recycled Paper

www.ingramcontent.com/pod-product-compliance
Lightning Source LLC
Chambersburg PA
CBHW080538290526
45790CB00006B/2453